Conten

Map of Thanet
Introduction 03

Margate	**04**
24 Hours in Margate	06
Food & Drink	07
Shopping	13
See & Do	17
Stay	23

Broadstairs	**26**
24 Hours in Broadstairs	28
Food & Drink	29
See & Do	32
Shopping	33
Stay	37

Ramsgate	**40**
24 Hours in Ramsgate	42
Food & Drink	43
Shopping	51
See & Do	52
Stay	53

Elsewhere	**54**
Food & Drink	55
Shopping	57
See & Do	58

All go in Margate
Old Town 12
Dreaming of Dreamland 20
Ann Carrington's Thanet 24
99 problems but
a beach ain't one 34
Festivals and events 38
Thanet dining:
we're getting there 46

Transport **60**
Contributors **62**
Notes **65**

Thanet

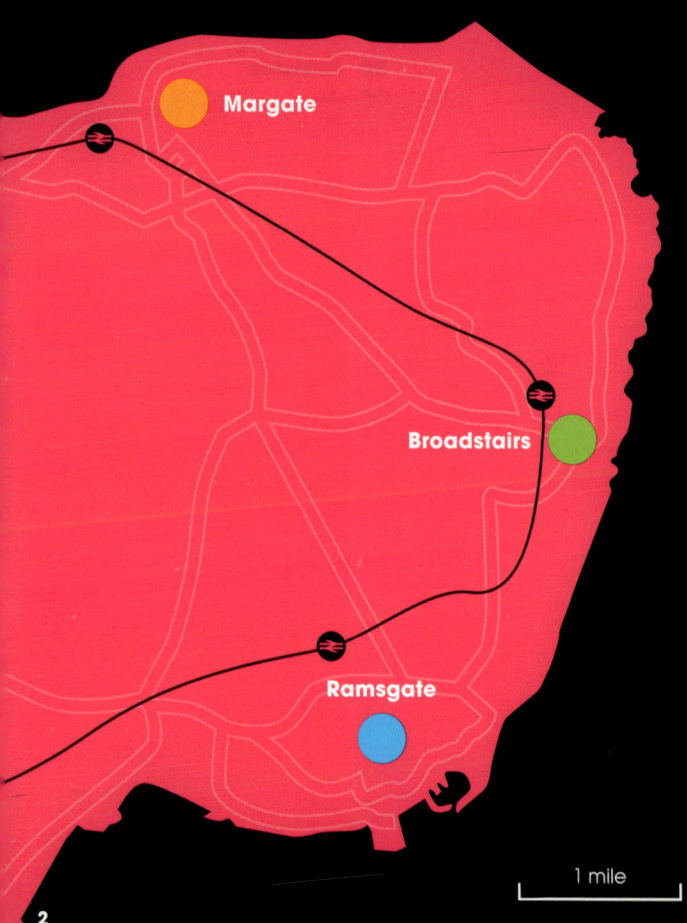

Introduction

The seductive sounds of the samba in Rio de Janeiro, the snow-capped mountains of Hokkaido in Japan and, er, Thanet. It's fair to say more than a few eyebrows were raised when travel experts Frommers listed this tiny stretch of the East Kent coast, once separated from the mainland, among 2011's must-see destinations.

But write off the Isle at your peril – exciting things are happening here. Scratch the surface, ditch your preconceptions, and it's easy to see why it's been attracting tourists for over 250 years.

We've aimed to unite Thanet's three main towns into one destination. It'd be a tragedy to travel all the way to Margate to visit the Turner Contemporary without taking a detour up the coast to experience the Victorian seaside charm of Broadstairs, perhaps rounding off your day with dinner in one of Ramsgate's wonderful restaurants. And it's all too easy to overlook the hidden gems you'll find in villages like Westgate on Sea and Birchington. Thanet's small, so make sure you see it all.

Discover Thanet in no way sets out to be an exhaustive guide to the Isle. Instead we want to showcase the very best of Margate, Broadstairs and Ramsgate. This is Thanet's finest, carefully picked by a bunch of knowledgeable insiders to prevent your day trip or weekend away being soured by a dodgy sandwich in a ropey seaside caff, or ruined by a wasted hour at some half-baked tourist attraction. We're independently published meaning we can tell it exactly like it is.

So pop this in your pocket and go and Discover Thanet.

Stewart Turner, Editor

Margate

Mention Margate to anyone of a certain age and they'll picture kiss-me-quick hats, seafront amusements, neon, and raunchy postcards. Being of the same generation as Margate's most famous daughter, I too have Tracey Emin's memories of the rollercoaster and big wheel, the place packed with day-trippers, eating candy floss and chips.

In my teens, hanging round Dreamland was a hot night out, the funfair and bright lights giving the place an air of adventure and tawdry romance. Now with much of that gone, Margate has had to find a new identity and it is emerging well. Arty, edgy, and with a pleasing verve, there is something raw and compelling about what is rising from the ashes.

Art is the big thing with small galleries springing up as well as the flagship Turner Contemporary. The interesting mix of new entrepreneurs, the bohemian and born-and-breds hasn't always sat happily together, but it has resulted in passions that will take the town far. The Harbour Arm has been revitalised and is the perfect vantage point to appreciate the glorious sunsets, luminous light and big skies so often forgotten, and the delightful Old Town is coming up with new tricks all the time. If once this part of Thanet was tagged Benefits-on-Sea, now it should be labelled: Watch this space…

Jane Wenham-Jones

© Dave Mason

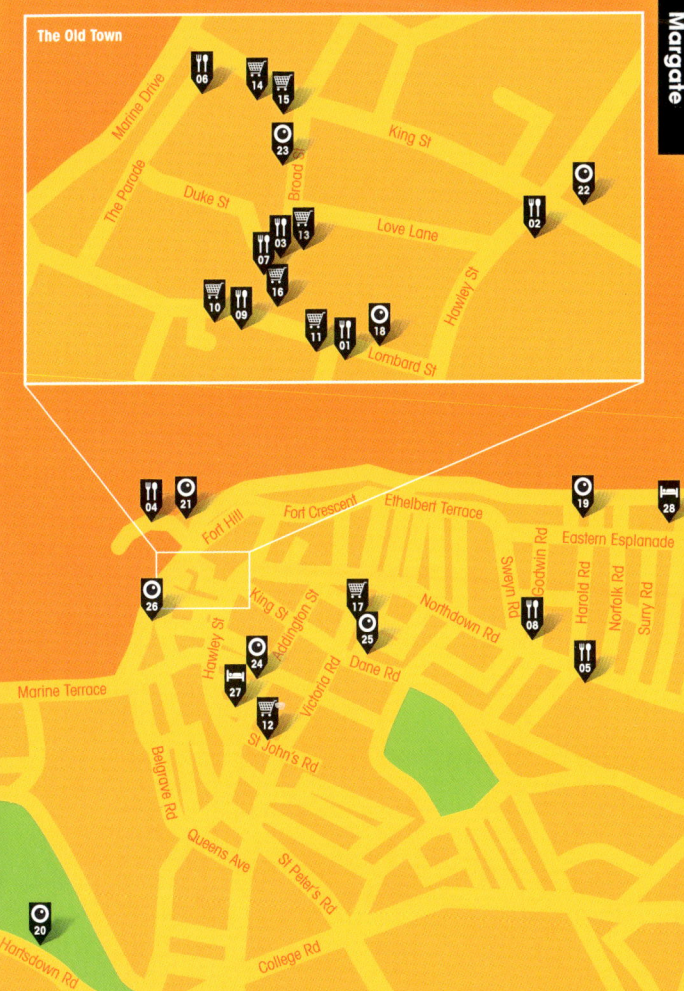

24 hours in Margate

Discover Thanet editor Stewart Turner reveals how to make the most of Margate.

Morning. OK, so Arlington House isn't the best introduction to Margate. A grubby, brutalist tower block that greets first-time visitors with something akin to a punch in the face, the general consensus seems to be it'd be better off razed to the ground. But take a few minutes to appreciate it. If this beast lived in London it'd be cooed over, listed, and photographed for a coffee table book. If you can get inside for a look at the sweeping views from the upper floor flats, even better.

Cross the road to take a pew at the Nayland Rock Shelter, the place where TS Eliot wrote The Wasteland, before that inevitable trip to the spanking new Turner Contemporary (see **21**, page 18). Then take a stroll around the Old Town's various shops and galleries before heading up the hill to Cliftonville. Don't be put off by the tatty facades of the buildings that run along the sea front – 100 years ago this was one of the finest places to live in the country, a smart suburb where the well-to-do headed in droves to escape the oiks down the road in Margate.

Stop at the Lido for a quick photo opportunity at the gloriously kitsch sign, then take a right down Dalby Square – immortalised on film in a feature length Only Fools & Horses episode. Mrs Baker's Sunny Sea Guest House was located at number 32.

Lunch. Stop for a spot of lunch among the glamorous ladies at Batchelor's Patisserie. And don't forget to save room for some of those lovingly crafted petit fours (see **05**, page 9).

Afternoon. Head down Northdown Road, popping into the assorted second hand furniture shops on the way. Rest assured, among the faux-leather sofas and rusting fridge-freezers, there are bargains to be had. If you're still empty-handed, about turn and head to RG Scott's (see **17**, page 16), a treasure trove of antiques, reclaimed furniture and curiosities. And speaking of curiosities, you're just around the corner from the Shell Grotto (see **25**, page 22).

Evening. Michelin-recommended cuisine in Margate? It's true. Head back down Northdown Road to sample some of Dev Biswal's brilliantly executed Indian food at The Ambrette (see **02**, page 8). Just don't ask for a Chicken Bhuna. If that sounds a little too formal, head to The Lifeboat (see **09**, page 11) and have your fill of local seafood, sausages and pies washed down with some potent local ales.

Sleep. Head to the Reading Rooms, a luxurious B&B on Georgian Hawley Square. It's by far the best place to stay in Margate.

Food & Drink

© DT

01 The Mad Hatter's

Peter Clements-Bullett *is* the Mad Hatter, inhabiting his curious and delightful tearooms with an air of distracted loucheness and jauntily sported top hat. Complete with tinsel, because in Peter's world it's forever Christmas. His temple to Victoriana is plastered with vaguely spooky antique photos (that rabbit: brrr), tributes to Princess Di and a carnival of Christmas decorations. But it's not all eccentricity: home-baked cakes are first class and tea is served properly from vintage porcelain. If you're lucky, Peter might show you his modelling photos: brooding in Monaco or groovy-man on the Portobello Road. Truly a one-off. *(MO'L)*

9 Lombard Street, Margate CT9 1EJ
T: 01843 232 626
Open Saturdays only

Margate

02 The Ambrette

Dev Biswal's contemporary Indian cooking in the converted St George's Hotel boozer has impressed since it first opened its doors. Word of something special spread fast amongst Isle natives, with major critics and guides – including Michelin – following in their wake. Dev's regularly changing menu makes great use of Kent's wonderful produce in intricate dishes like belly ribs of Kentish pork (unusual on an Indian menu) flavoured with fennel and sesame seeds. His dhosas are divine. Perhaps he might invest a little more in the Ambrette's interior, but there's no mistaking the passion on the plate. *(MO'L)*

44 King Street, Margate CT9 1QE
T: 01843 231 504
TheAmbrette.co.uk
Closed Mondays

03 The Cupcake Café

'Keep Calm and Have a Cup Cake' is advice well worth following, and a selection of beautifully crafted cakes in a wide range of flavours like lemon & lavender, coffee & walnut and chocolate & lime makes it all the wiser. Set in a beautiful glass-fronted shop in the heart of the Old Town, you're spoilt for choice between delightfully decorated cakes to home cooked toasties and stews. The menu is simple, wholesome and excellent value. Perfect for a take-away sugar rush, or a light snack while ploughing through the weekend newspapers. *(A-MN)*

4-5 Market Place, Margate CT9 1ER
T: 01843 231 300
TheCupcake.biz

04 The Harbour Arm

Margate's 19th century stone pier – The Harbour Arm in new money – is the perfect place to wind down after all that art appreciation over at the Turner Contemporary. The first place you come to is BeBeached, run by Jean, passionate about all things local. The menu is full of hearty, wholesome, well-cooked food, including some of the best vegetarian options on the Isle. The Lighthouse Bar has arguably the best views in Margate, and the colourful hire bikes at Caitlin's Beach Cruisers are perfect for nipping along to Broadstairs and Ramsgate up the coast. Look out for events and exhibitions in the studio spaces too. *(A-MN)*

The Harbour Arm, Margate CT9 1AP
MargateHarbourArm.co.uk

© DT

05 Batchelor's Patisserie

With its Formica tables and unapologetically beige decor, Batchelor's has found itself in the midst of a revival. Take a seat amongst the blue rinsed old ladies and treat yourself to a teacake, scone or one of those delightfully dainty petit fours – all freshly made in the bakery at the back of the shop. Wash it down with a milky coffee and close your eyes; you can almost see the Vespas and Lambrettas pulling up outside. If you're in too much of a hurry to stay, it's also the perfect place to grab a cake for that special occasion. *(A-MN)*

246 Northdown Road, Cliftonville CT9 2PX
T: 01843 221 227
Closed Sundays & Mondays

Margate

06 Harbour Café

Fancy flexing your jazz hands over a spot of supper? The Harbour Café doubles up as Vortex-on-Sea, little sister to the celebrated hangout of London's assorted chin-strokers. An early pioneer of Margate's revival, the Harbour Café has weathered more than its fair share of wet January weekends, serving up decent coffee and a nice selection of cakes within its stylish, tiled interior. While the menu is a little overdue an overhaul, it's a great spot for a long lunch or supper, and the delicious homemade burger is undoubtedly the best in Margate. *(ST)*

10 Royal York Mansions, The Parade, Margate CT9 1EZ
T: 01843 290 110
Closed Mondays

07 The Greedy Cow

It's a long way from the kitchens of 5 star hotels to this little Old Town space, but that's the journey chef Pete Hunt has taken. In their 'deli and eatery', he and wife Rachel – originally from Margate and lured back by the town's blossoming – are specialising in cheeses, many from Kent or Sussex: buttery Winterdale Shaw, maybe, or piquant Kentish Blue. Juices, breads (from Whitstable bakery, Slow Bread), and even crisps are local. In summer, they're doing picnic boxes for the beach. The cool, creamy shop/café is hung with vintage cow prints. Delicious. *(MO'L)*

3 Market Place, Margate CT9 1ER
T: 01843 447 557
GreedyCowDeli.com

08 Godwin

Given the girth-expanding size of the portions dished up at this family run chippy, it's a miracle they manage to stay in business. Steer clear of the chip shops half a mile up the road in Margate town centre, and take a detour to Cliftonville to sample some of the best fish and chips in Thanet. It's always a good sign if you have to wait ten minutes for your order, and sure enough you'll be rewarded with a satisfyingly crisp batter, succulent fresh fish and a veritable mountain of expertly fried chips. Be sure to sample one of their perfect pea fritters too. *(ST)*

71-73 Godwin Road, Cliftonville CT9 2HE
T: 01843 298 146
Closed Sundays and Monday lunchtime

© DS

09 The Lifeboat

An oasis for real ale lovers amid the decidedly more edgy hostelries lining the surrounding streets of the Old Town, The Lifeboat stocks a wide, constantly changing range of local brews from the likes of Gadds, Goachers and Hopdaemon, alongside eye-wateringly strong ciders and a couple of decent wines. The solid, locally sourced food on offer includes huge slabs of Kentish cheese with homemade chutneys, fresh lobster, and tasty Ramsgate sausages. Drop in on a Friday and have a punt on the seafood raffle, or look out for occasional live music events as varied as organ-driven jazz groups and local Hurdy Gurdy players. *(ST)*

1 Market Street, Margate, CT9 1EU
T: 07837 024 259
TheLifeboat-Margate.com

11

All go in Margate Old Town

Qing's Anne-Marie Nixey celebrates the renaissance of Margate's oldest streets.

Say "Margate" and what do you think of? Sandy beaches and the scenic railway? Sharply tailored suits and scooters? Maybe even bedsits? But walk back past the sea front, down the small alleyways with their flint cottages and you will discover a part of Margate that could change your image completely.

Margate Old Town started its journey as a little fishing hamlet back in the 17th century with tiny, one storey dwellings that you can still see today. Its close proximity to mainland Europe meant that entrepreneurial spirit flourished. The Dutch plundered the area near Alkali Row for ingredients to make pottery, Francis Cobb opened up a bank and a pub, and Cecil Square was the first formal square to spring up outside London.

The good times continued: Nelson wooed Lady Hamilton at her house on Hawley Square, Turner and Eliot passed through and made their indelible mark on the town, and even well into the mid-20th century this was a fashionable place to be. The blue plaque above the door at The Bull's Head commemorates Eric Morecombe's wedding reception, and Hattie Jacques lived with John Le Mesurier just around the corner. Not bad for a place the size of a small village.

The harder times are well documented. The past few years have seen Margate topping the league tables when it comes to high street vacancy rates. But far from rolling over and conking out, the Old Town has seized on this to become a melting pot of small, quirky boutiques and shops – a place pleasingly bereft of a branch of Starbucks or a Costa Coffee. For now. It's a movement that's come from the bottom up, with enterprising traders kick-starting a revival that looks set to last.

People from near and far are beginning to rediscover the backstreets, shops are being snapped up and lives are starting afresh. New galleries like Outside the Square, The Pie Factory and I Scream and Rock are bringing in art lovers from all over the UK. There's vintage a go-go with Betty B's and Helter Skelter, and finely-crafted pieces of originality and beauty at Qing, Margate Gallery and Blackbird.

Individuals with a passion for their craft are flocking to a place where there is camaraderie, enthusiasm and a chance to build something positive. It's an exciting time, and new friendships and alliances being formed. A phoenix rising from the ashes to once again put Margate firmly on the map.

Shopping

10 Madam Popoff

Squint hard enough on a Saturday afternoon on Market Street as Madam Popoff (aka Deborah Ellis) photographs a stick-thin model and you could almost be on the Kings Road, Chelsea circa 1967. This is Thanet's very own version of a beat boutique, full of fab gear from the 1960s and onwards, further cementing Margate's reputation as a Mecca for vintage shopping. The Madam's gone from strength to strength since hopping into bed with online retail giants ASOS, but this is your chance to get first dibs on the good stuff before it heads off the Isle by First Class post. *(ST)*
3 Market Street, Margate CT9 1EU
T: 01843 447 434
Closed Mondays

11 Helter Skelter Boutique

The Helter Skelter Boutique's twist on Margate's booming trend for vintage shopping is giving the stock room to breathe – no tiresome piles of clutter or daunting racks of vintage clothing to be found here. Whether you're looking to furnish your home with some stunning 1960s Italian light fittings and classic Ercol and G Plan furniture, or you're overwhelmed with the sudden urge to shield yourself from the Margate weather with a pair of vintage Ray bans or a sharp Gabbici cardigan, this is the place to pick them up. *(ST)*
13 Market Place, Margate CT9 1ES
T: 01843 223 474
HelterSkelterBoutique.com
Closed Sunday – Wednesday

12 Fontaine

Hidden away on a back street behind the smart Georgian splendour of Hawley Square you'll find one of Margate's finest buildings. It was originally built as a training school for maids, and more recently used as a MIND day centre, but Stuart Atkinson and Kiel Shaw have breathed new life into the place with an antiques showroom every bit as stunning as the structure that houses it. Full of classy French and English decorative antiques, alongside more recent pieces like chrome and smoked glass 1970s coffee tables and industrial light fittings, it's a wonderfully stylish addition to the Isle. *(ST)*
The Old Laundry, St John's Road,
Margate CT9 1LU
T: 01843 220 974
FontaineDecorative.com
Call ahead for opening times

Margate

© Niko Kolios

13 Qing
Qing is a dazzlingly pretty shop groaning with gorgeous goodies from China and the East, from impulse buys to desirable furniture. The owners have lived and worked in China, and source their quality products from individual designers and craftsmen that they know and trust. Soft furnishings like colourful satin and silk throws and delicate Oriental lighting vie for space alongside some of the most stunning furniture you're ever likely to see – beautifully distressed lacquerware in strikingly bold colours. You can even have something made to order, too. The prices are reasonable and the quality is undisputable. *(ST)*

7 Market Place, Margate CT9 1EN
T: 01843 299 055
QingArt.co.uk
Closed Wednesdays

Margate

14 Etcetera

Over Etcetera's two floors you'll find all manner of vintage, retro and industrial design classics, from larger items of furniture like Danish sideboards and stripped metal desks down to original Jielde lamps and GPO phones. The range and quality of Etcetera's goods easily rivals any equivalent London shop – but all with a Margate price tag. And don't panic if you're worried about getting your brand new teak dining table home on the train, Etcetera makes regular deliveries to London and the rest of the UK. *(GH)*
4 King Street, Margate CT9 1DA
T: 07977 161 915
Etcetera-Online.co.uk
Open Wednesday – Saturday

15 Betty B's

Harking back to the heady days when teddy boys teased their gravity-defying quiffs in the curved glass windows of Margate Old Town, Betty B's lives in a world forever populated with buxom blonde bombshells, Dansette record players and the Wurlitzer jukebox. The suitably retro chessboard floor is piled high with period outfits, vintage posters, and Bakelite design classics from the '40s and '50s. If none of that floats your boat, it's worth popping in for a look at the wonderful Margate tourism films on the screen in the corner of the shop. *(ST)*
9 King Street, Margate CT9 1HB
T: 07974 533 439
Open Thursday – Saturday

16 Blackbird

Blackbird, the creation of textile designer Maxine Sutton, is so much more than just a shop. With sewing and screenprinting workshops on the two floors upstairs, it allows you the chance to realise your talents under careful guidance, or just buy handmade pieces, like a divine 'Pugs not Drugs' bag or one of Emily Warren's papier-mâché busts for your wall, from the beautiful shop on the ground floor. Maxine's intimate knowledge of each piece and the maker behind it reveals the passion she has for recycling, making, creating and pushing the boundaries in design. *(A-MN)*
2 Market Place, Margate CT9 1ER
T: 01843 229 553
Blackbird-England.com
Open Thursday – Saturday

15

© DT

17 R G Scott's

Housed in a wonderful old ice cream factory, Scott's is the kind of place where it's all too easy to spend an entire afternoon. There are three sprawling floors of antique furniture and bygones to browse, battered oil paintings, school chairs, vintage clocks, rusty old companion sets, and drawers packed with every kind of knob and knocker you could possibly imagine. Try Junk Deluxe in the basement if you want to pick up Tretchikoff's Green Lady or a sunburst wall clock for your living room wall. The whole gloriously dusty shebang is overseen by Ronnie himself – resplendent in an oversized Stetson hat. *(ST)*

Grotto Hill, Margate CT9 2BU
T: 01843 220 653
ScottsMargate.co.uk
Closed Wednesdays and Sundays

See & Do

18 Margate Gallery

The light and airy Margate Gallery hosts an ever-changing selection of prints, sculptures and furniture from local, national and international artists. They include the Isle's very own Zoe Murphy, whose highly sought-after furniture and textiles have a distinctly Margate feel, and illustrator Andy Touhy, whose bold prints of local landmarks make a nostalgic nod at the iconic railway and travel posters of the past. Janet also offers a bespoke art consultancy service, allowing potential buyers to view artworks in their own home, and participates in the Own Art scheme, making art affordable via an interest-free loan from the Arts Council. *(A-MN)*
2 Lombard Street, Margate CT9 1EJ
T: 01843 292 779
MargateGallery.co.uk
Closed Monday – Wednesday

19 Tom Thumb Theatre

With just sixty shabby red velour seats tucked away in an old Victorian coach house, the Tom Thumb is one of the smallest theatres in the country. Opened as a theatre in the 1980s, it's now run by a devoted family who put on anything from stand-up comedy to storytelling evenings and live music in a unique atmosphere of faded charm. Tickets are cheap, the atmosphere's intimate and there's often a chance to go drinking with the cast afterwards. No waiting outside to get an autograph here! *(A-MN)*
Eastern Esplanade, Cliftonville CT9 2LB
T: 01843 221 791
TomThumbTheatre.co.uk

20 Margate FC

Margate's Ryman League minnows have a rich and bizarre history, the highlight of which was a plum FA Cup tie against Spurs in the early '70s in front of some 14,000 giddy spectators. After a brief spell playing as Thanet United in the 1980s and a few heady years in the '90s sponsored by one-time Margate resident Buster Bloodvessel's Bad Manners, 2011 sees them languishing in non-league mediocrity. Nevertheless, invest a tenner on a Saturday afternoon at the Hartsdown and you'll experience an afternoon of real, unreconstructed football – a world away from the prawn sandwiches and hospitality suites of Gate's big city cousins. *(ST)*
Hartsdown Park, Hartsdown Road,
Margate CT9 5QZ
T: 01843 221 769
Margate-FC.com

17

Margate

© DS

21 Turner Contemporary 12/05/12 08/09/12

Loved and scorned in equal measure, David Chipperfield's striking milky-white building makes no apology for what it brings to Margate. Anchored between the sea and town on the exact site of Mrs Booth's house where Turner used to stay, it frames the dramatic northern sunsets with which he became synonymous. The inaugural exhibition centres on Turner's awe inspiring yet little-known painting The Eruption of the Souffrier Mountain, and the first major show of his work follows hot on its heels in January 2012. A historic transformation to a down-at-heel seaside town, the Turner Contemporary is the jolt in the arm that Margate's been waiting for. *(A-MN)*

The Rendezvous, Margate CT9 1HG
T: 01843 233 000
TurnerContemporary.org

22 The Tudor House

It's not all Georgian, Victorian and David Chipperfield in Margate, you know. Blink and you'll miss this quiet, unassuming house just around from The Ambrette on the corner of King Street. Built in 1525, it's one of the oldest buildings on the Isle, with a rich pedigree of owners including pioneering brewer and banker Francis Cobb. Part of the exterior was even plastered over until the fifties before it was completely restored by a sympathetic owner. Open rather infrequently, but well worth a detour while you're exploring the Old Town. *(A-MN)*
King Street, Margate CT9 1QE

23 The Pie Factory

The neglected pork butcher's in Broad Street has been brought back to life by locals Janet and Tim Williams. With their ethos of providing good quality affordable studio and exhibition space it comprises of three gorgeous galleries, artist studios, Margate's first pop up shop and a smart new café that is set to bring pies back to The Pie Factory. Restored sympathetically, letting the building speak for itself, it is the perfect backdrop for artists to promote their work. Look out for regular open studios for a chance to admire the beautiful rooftop terrace, too. *(A-MN)*
5-7 Broad Street, Margate CT9 1EW
T: 07879 630 257
PieFactoryMargate.co.uk

24 Theatre Royal

Pick up the Theatre Royal and put it in the middle of London's West End and it wouldn't look out of place. Opened in 1787, this is actually the second oldest theatre in the country and has played host to thousands of legendary luvvies including Charlie Chaplin and Julie Andrews. Inside you'll find a satisfying mixture of grandeur and intimacy. Take a little time to savour the building's Georgian character and have a look for Charlie the ghost during the interval. Artistic director Will Wollen leaves no cultural stone unturned – from Shakespeare to the Gang Show, Opera to Panto, and everything imaginable in between. *(JM)*
Addington Street, Margate CT9 1PW
T: 0845 130 1786
TheatreRoyalMargate.com

Dreaming of Dreamland

Big plans are in place for Margate's iconic theme park, as Iain Aitch explains.

The news that Margate's Dreamland theme park was to be revamped and re-opened may have brought a warm nostalgic glow for many, conjuring up memories of candyfloss, dizzying Waltzer rides and stolen kisses. For me, though, the announcement that Dreamland has received the nod and funding to help it become a heritage theme park brings together a wonderful mixture of childhood memories and family history.

Based around the old funfair's 1920 Grade II-listed Scenic Railway, the new Dreamland will be a working homage to a slice of Britain's cultural history, with classic rides having been purchased from similar small theme parks around the country as they have closed. Names like the Water Chute, Caterpillar and River Caves are tantalising for someone who grew up in Margate when Dreamland boasted identical rides, as I did.

But they also bring back memories of my grandfather, who started work at Dreamland upon arriving home from World War II. He stayed until he retired some 30 years later, taking the somewhat unorthodox career path from catering worker to chief engineer.

In retrospect I realise that my grandfather spent most days up to his elbows in grease, but his job seemed endlessly glamorous to me. After all, this was the place that I loved most in the world. I saved up pocket money in anticipation of Dreamland opening for the season, guarding the free ride tickets that my grandfather sometimes gave me, as if they were winning lottery tickets. Even before I reached the gates I had planned what rides I intended to go on and in which order. When Dreamland became a pay-to-enter theme park in the early 1980s I would find sneaky ways to get in without paying, sharing an entrance hand stamp between several friends. Even football stickers, arcade games and sweets were no competition for any ride onsite.

My grandfather's casual Sunday lunchtime revelation that he took the Scenic Railway out for a test spin most mornings was akin to his telling me that he was actually Evel Knievel or that he played centre forward for England on his day off. This unique ride is a far cry from today's roller coasters, controlled as it is by an onboard brakeman precariously perched at the middle of the train. To us kids the brakemen were death-defying daredevils, so this was something to brag about in the playground.

Rides destined for Dreamland are safely in storage around the country, but there is still a lot of work to do before visitors can take a stroll down memory lane or show their grandchildren how thrilling rides such as the Whip or the wooden Wild Mouse can be.

Far from being a dry historical monument, the new Dreamland is set to be a place that lives up to its name, mixing the smell of diesel with the feeding of the imagination and that bit in your stomach that flips over in fear or in objection to the rules of gravity.

There are also plans to renovate the façade of Margate's wonderful Art Deco Dreamland cinema, with phase two of the project possibly including the transformation of its auditorium into a museum of youth culture. The listed building will bring the pop cultural history of teddy boys, mods, rockers, punks, skinheads and soul boys back to life, as well as acting as a hub for those creating the youth culture of the future. Dreamland may be the populist sibling of the Turner Contemporary, but it will be every bit as important to the future of the town.

Within the next five years I shall hopefully be viewing the map of the finished heritage park and once again planning the order in which to visit the rides, with a childish glee and a nod to my grandfather's memory.

To keep up to date with the project visit DreamlandMargate.com.

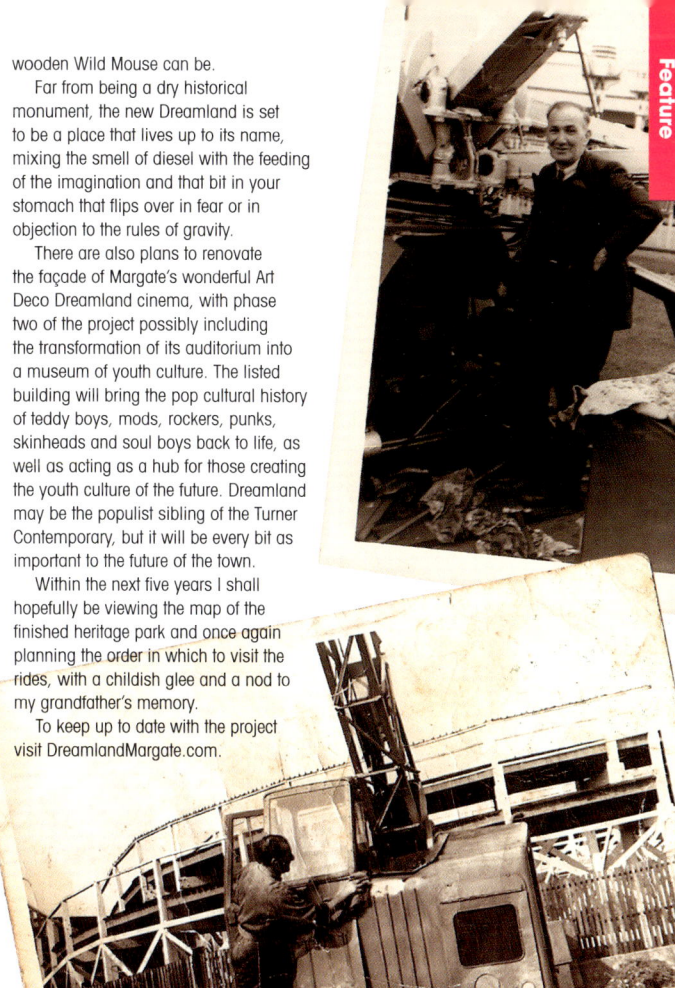

Margate

25 Shell Grotto

The Shell Grotto is Thanet's very own underground Stonehenge, a much-loved curiosity whose origins may never be solved. A series of underground passages carved into solid chalk, the walls are decorated with over 4 million shells arranged in obscure patterns and symbols. The grotto was discovered by accident in 1835 when James Newlove somewhat irresponsibly lowered his son into a hole he discovered while digging a duck pond. Prehistoric temple or Victorian folly? No one knows, but one thing's certain: there's nowhere like this anywhere else in the world. *(GH)*

Grotto Hill, Margate CT9 2BU
T: 01843 220 008
ShellGrotto.co.uk
Open weekends only during winter

26 Art For All

Art For All's children's pottery sessions and school holiday workshops are the kind of events that inspire hushed silence, as once-squabbling kids suddenly sit side-by-side engrossed in their work. Workshops generally have a theme, a recent hit being a Turner inspired session where a local artist helped enraptured children recreate one of the great man's landscapes using watercolours. You can even pick up a take-away craft set for the beach if the weather's too good to be indoors. Located right on the front with views across the sea, it's a godsend for parents with creative children. *(AS)*
9-10 Marine Drive, Margate CT9 1DH
T: 07878 776 196
ArtForAll.eu

Stay

27 Reading Rooms

Since swinging open its doors back in 2009, this elegant Grade II-listed Georgian townhouse has sent the nation's travel writers weak at the knees, winning a place in the coveted Mr & Mrs Smith directory in the process. Even notoriously fussy TV hotelier Ruth Watson was won over during its appearance on her Channel 4 series, despite much huffing and puffing along the way. The delicious, locally sourced breakfast is served straight to your room, saving you that depressing trudge down to a basement dining room and providing a little more time to enjoy the huge rococo bed. It's by far the most sumptuous place to stay in Margate. *(ST)*
31 Hawley Square, Margate CT9 1PH
T: 01843 225 166
TheReadingRoomsMargate.co.uk

28 Walpole Bay Hotel

This grand old Edwardian hotel is where Margate's most famous daughter Tracy Emin stays whenever she's in town, no doubt attracted by the quirky surroundings and eccentric clutter, not to mention the stunning 1927 Otis trellis gated lift in reception. The Walpole also doubles up as a 'living museum', with dusty antiques and curios filling every nook and cranny of the hotel's rooms and corridors. Stay for a three course Sunday lunch and you'll be greeted by the somewhat surreal sight of the resident pianist caressing the keys of a 1908 pianola. While the food's a little ordinary, the atmosphere is anything but. *(ST)*
Fifth Avenue, Cliftonville CT9 2JJ
T: 01843 221 703
WalpoleBayHotel.co.uk

Ann Carrington's Thanet

The internationally acclaimed artist takes us on a personal tour of the Isle's thriving art scene.

It's five years since I moved down to Thanet from East London, and I know I made the right decision. Of course, as an artist I was aware of the exciting plans for Turner Contemporary, now completed and opening its doors to the public for the first time. But I had also heard, through friends and fellow artists, about the regeneration of a place that for so long had been regarded as something of a backwater of Kent, dreaming of its past glories.

Thanet has woken up to a new century, and a new way of looking at art. From the light flooded galleries of the Turner Contemporary, to the heart of Margate's Old Town, with its eclectic mix of small studios, galleries and work spaces, the Isle exudes the edgy individuality of a place where great things are happening. A place where artists, both established and emerging, work together in premises with histories every bit as unique and fascinating as the art being created there.

The Pie Factory, on Broad Street, is one of my favourite places. A pork butcher's from 1847 right up until the 1970s, it's been transformed into an exciting mix of workshops, galleries and performance spaces. Katie Welsford, an artist I have long admired, occupies one of the Pie Factory studios. Her work is a fascinating mix of sculpture, fashion and jewellery design, exhibited both in the UK and Europe. Katie feels a strong loyalty to Thanet, having been the director of the hugely successful Margate Rocks Art and Ecology festival a couple of years ago.

Just around the corner from the Pie Factory is the Community Pharmacy Gallery. This listed Georgian building houses Beeping Bush, a not for profit community arts and digital media organisation, which has actively encouraged art growth on the Isle, establishing a vibrant networking hub for the area.

At the centre of Margate's creative activity is Limbo, housed in an old, disused electricity substation. It's a brutally utilitarian yet somehow engaging building, positively buzzing with ideas. New curators Jim Lockey and Katy Norton are about to pick up where last year's hugely successful and innovative 'Dead Season Live Art' left off. Paul Hazelton, internationally recognised for his unique and intricate sculptures fashioned from the detritus of human and animal life, also has a studio here. Paul is very much a part of the Limbo team and the Thanet art community.

The Isle's three main towns, Margate, Broadstairs and Ramsgate, are all involved in the regeneration process and all have distinct personalities. I have made my home in Broadstairs, whilst my friend and fellow artist Shelly Goldsmith, whose textile work has won awards both in the UK and internationally, lives a short walk along the coast in Ramsgate.

I love the 'rawness' of the art scene here – the old industrial and commercial buildings dragged out of their boarded up decay into the light of a new age of artistic endeavour. My own Margate studio is surrounded by warehouses and damaged cars hopefully awaiting their own 'regeneration'. The established artists are here to encourage and add gravitas to the outrageous and courageous ideas of the young newcomers. Thanet is full of contrasts, old and new, creative and industrial, towns and beaches, light and shade – and I'm grateful to be a part of it.

More Art on the Isle

There are plenty of hidden art studios on the Isle. Look out for **Meltdowns** in Ramsgate, Sarah Craske & Stephen Melton's studios and project space with an extensive and inspirational programme of classes and workshops. **Julie Westbury**, Ramsgate-based artist, regularly exhibits her kaleidoscopic photo collages at Nice Things, while **Jenny Duff** makes highly desirable melamine tableware, producing bold, colourful coasters and placemats. Back in Margate, **Marine Studios** houses regular talks and exhibitions from a Grade II-listed building overlooking the main sands, and **Zoe Murphy** crafts her seaside-inspired furniture and textiles from her studio at the Pie Factory. *(ST)*

The Pie Factory,
5-9 Broad Street, Margate CT9 1EW
T: 07879 630 257
PieFactoryMargate.co.uk

Community Pharmacy Gallery,
16 Market Place, Margate CT9 1ES
T: 01843 223 800
BeepingBush.co.uk

Limbo, The Substation Project Space,
Margate CT9 1DX
T: 07812 780 984
LimboArts.co.uk

© Paul Hazelton

Broadstairs

Of the three main towns of Thanet, this is the cute one. Other beaches may be more dramatic and sweeping, but Viking Bay has the biggest ahhh factor, whether it's twinkling at night or picture-book pretty with its fishing boats bobbing by day. Reminiscent of Cornish hideaways, much of the town's aesthetic appeal is in the curve of the bay, its natural symmetry and sloping streets.

Broadstairs is a place of timeless charm and traditional seaside trappings of Punch & Judy, Italian ice-cream parlours and seriously good fish and chips. The locals – both from Broadstairs itself and the adjoining village of St Peters – are an eclectic, eccentric bunch ranging from the retired, old school dyed-in-the-wool stalwarts of Middle England to arty dilettantes and table-thumping thorns in the council's side.

There are as many poetry readings, live music sessions and theatre productions – don't miss the annual Dickens Play – as there are Progressive Dinners and good works by the Rotary Club. The pubs are the old-fashioned sort, boasting colourful regulars with opinions to share. Gossips flourish in Broadstairs.

It's a town best balanced with trips to The Smoke to catch up with the rest of the world, but after all these years, I can still wander the twisting pathway behind Bleak House where the great man penned part of David Copperfield and think: "Wow. I live here."

Jane Wenham-Jones

© Aaron Stone

24 hours in Broadstairs

Kiki Case, editor of *Isle Magazine*, reveals how to get the best out of a day in Broadstairs.

9.45am. St Peter's Village Tour
Even if guided tours are not your thing, this award-winning – and free – tour of St Peter's village in Broadstairs is an experience not to be missed. A black-robed monk greets you in the gloomy porch of the Saxon church, soldiers from the Napoleonic wars challenge you, Victorian workhouse masters tell you about life for the poor and the infamous smuggler Joss Snelling boasts about his exploits.

Thursdays and some Saturdays, April – December. Call 07546 514 948 or visit VillageTour.co.uk. Though free, booking is essential.

Lunch. Osteria Pizzeria Posillipo
It's worth going to this popular Italian for the view alone, but be sure to book a table on the terrace overlooking the sea. On a bright sunny day, you could be forgiven for thinking you're on the Italian Riviera. (see **30**, page 30)

Afternoon.
Work off your lunch with a leisurely stroll and you'll discover that Broadstairs still retains much of its Victorian charm. Charles Dickens was a regular visitor and extolled the virtues of the town as 'our English watering place'.

Face the promenade, and to the right you will see the bandstand, where regular concerts take you back to the British seaside's heyday. Wander to the left and you'll see Regency and Victorian influences in the gorgeous architecture on one side and Viking Bay with its quaint harbour and pier on the other. Follow the cobbled streets up to Bleak House, used by Dickens as a holiday home, Union Square, an area steeped in smuggling legend, and Church Square, where the extremely rare surviving wash houses are a reminder of the practice of washing dirty linen in public.

Walk down Albion Street and stop off at the Albion bookshop to browse through the unruly piles of second-hand books. When you've had enough of walking, buy a bottle of chilled champagne from The Bottleneck, take it down to the beach, kick your shoes off in the sand and enjoy!

Dinner. Peen's Gastro Bar
For good gastro grub, sit at the splendid continental-style bar at Peen's, and choose from the menu of modern British dishes. You might even find yourself tempted by the cocktails, which start at a very reasonable £4.50. (see **31**, page 30)

Sleep.
Spend the night at Belvidere Place, a quirky and stylish boutique hotel, and enjoy its charming personal service and delicious breakfasts. (see **40**, page 37)

Food & Drink

Broadstairs

© DT

29 Oscar's Festival Café

Graham Ward's background as a successful artist shines through every atom of this delightful, tiny café, themed around the Festival of Britain. One major draw is a superb range of home-made cakes (coffee and walnut; fudgy brownies; gorgeously squelchy carrot) and local crab sandwiches, but there are home-made soups, savoury tarts and salads too. Plus lashings of ginger beer. Oscar's is so tiny, you often find yourself in conversation with the entire café, even those who spill out into the pretty back garden. People arrive at Oscar's as customers but frequently leave as friends. *(MO'L)*

15 Oscar Road, Broadstairs CT10 1QJ
T: 07595 750 091
OscarsFestivalCafe.co.uk
Open Thursday – Sunday

Broadstairs

30 Posillipo *(Cena 13/05/12)*

A firm favourite of none other than Antonio Carluccio, this buzzing family-run trattoria serves up some of the best pizza and pasta this side of Mount Vesuvius. The wood-fired pizzas are authentically Neapolitan, and the pasta menu makes fine use of locally caught seafood. Book well in advance for a table on the terrace overlooking Viking Bay in the summer months – just perfect for a long, lazy weekend lunch. Take a deep breath and let the often rather surly service fly over your head: while you certainly won't be treated like royalty at Posillipo, the food is majestic. *(ST)*
14 Albion Street, Broadstairs CT10 1LU
T: 01843 601 133
Posillipo.co.uk

31 Peen's Gastro Bar

This splendid continental-style bar dishes up some of Broadstairs' best gastro-grub. Choose from a menu of modern British dishes (large tiger prawns, garlic, chilli & lemon; char-grilled 100% Kentish beef burger), with the odd nod to Europe (marinated pork kebab, baba ganoush, tzatziki, homemade flatbread; fish stew with tiger prawns, mussels, squid, saffron and local, seasonal white fish). The cuisine uses local produce, including seafood from the local crab man just two minutes down the road. You might even find yourself tempted by the cocktails, which start at a very reasonable £4.50. *(KC)*
Peen's, 8 Victoria Place,
Broadstairs CT10 1QS
T: 01843 861 289
PeensGastroBar.co.uk

32 Louisa Bay Café

I've been known to while away entire summers at this fabulous spot at the base of the cliffs on tiny Louisa Bay. New owners Camilla and Paul Naisbitt aren't blowing a winning formula: you'll still find the Isle's best bacon sandwich, terrific sausages, free-range egg and chips, and ice creams – not forgetting the famous coleslaw – but they're determined that everything's local where possible and of the highest quality. Whether it's for cakes and proper coffee in the afternoon, or lunch for ravenous, beach-weary children (there are buckets and spades, balls and shrimp nets too), this is one of the Isle's genuinely hidden gems. Open from March 'til late October, weather permitting. *(MO'L)*
Queens Gardens, Broadstairs CT10 1QE

© DT

33 Morelli's

Once our seaside towns bristled with cafés like Morelli's, but time and 'progress' have made them rarities. So we should treasure survivors as glorious as this one – opened in 1932, and refurbished in 1957 in the very height of Formica fabulousness. Retro fans boggle at the frankly bonkers ceiling relief, pink leatherette booths and backlit displays of sundaes and banana splits. There are cakes of varying levels of interest, and a selection of decent sandwiches, but the real draw is the home-made gelato, a family recipe and a thing of beauty: try amarena cherry, or simple 'plain ice' (Italian fior di latte). Unmissable. *(MO'L)*

14 Victoria Parade, Broadstairs CT10 1QS
T: 01843 862 500
MorellisGelato.com

34 Neptune's Hall

This traditional pub in the centre of Broadstairs was apparently mentioned in a Napoleonic murder trial, but luckily things are a lot more civilised in there nowadays. The Neptune's Hall is an excellent bet for a friendly welcome, good beer, especially if you like real ale, and a front row seat on much of the surrounding nightlife. There's regular live music, and a wonderful garden around the back for those balmy beery evenings. The pub is also famous locally for organising the annual New Year's Day dip, when the regulars brave the icy chill of the North Sea in the name of charity. *(JM)*

1-5 Harbour Street, Broadstairs CT10 1ET
T: 01843 861 400
NeptunesHall.co.uk

35 Nonna's Kitchen

Sisters Lucia Collins and Linda Berritt's Italian background can be tasted in every dish from this teeny, friendly outlet – they make all the food freshly to family recipes, and it shows. Whether it's a rich lasagne, creamy four cheeses or their popular arancini – deep-fried, stuffed risotto balls – it's all about the authenticity. Fancy one of their picnic bags to take to the beach? Nonna's is only minutes away. Cakes (including Italian specialties like cannolli and tiramisu) are homemade, and there are pizzas, baguettes, panini and salads too. Having a party? Let Nonna's do the cooking for you: easy. *(MO'L)*

1 Oscar Road, Broadstairs CT10 1QJ
T: 01843 579 799
NonnasKitchen.co.uk
Closed Sundays and evenings

See & Do

36 The Palace Cinema

The Palace Cinema (don't be surprised to hear it called <u>The Windsor</u>) is a local institution. Seating just 111 people, with a cute 23 seat balcony, it's housed in a Grade II listed building in the middle of Broadstairs. If you want to see the latest release in a friendly, independent cinema, with good value ticket prices, The Palace offers character and intimacy along with the usual features you'd get at one of those soulless out-of-town multiplexes. Look out for cult and arthouse offerings on Tuesdays courtesy of the Thanet Film Society (September – June) *(JM)*

Harbour Street, Broadstairs CT10 1ET
T: 01843 865 726
PalaceBroadstairs.co.uk
ThanetFilm.co.uk

Shopping

Broadstairs

37 Harrington's

Harrington's is like the ironmongers of your childhood, when staff wore brown work-coats and wrapped each individual screw in a paper bag. This wonderful shop's original double-front goes back for miles; ask for something not on display and one of the owner brothers will disappear into what seems to be a magical labyrinth. Nooks, crannies, a myriad of tiny drawers, a dazzling collection of domestic necessities – eat your heart out trendy pretenders like Labour and Wait. Rumoured to be the inspiration for The Two Ronnies' legendary 'Four Candles' sketch – Ronnie Corbett used to have a house on the Broadstairs seafront – it's a much-loved, living time capsule. *(MO'L)*
1 York Street, Broadstairs CT10 1PD
T: 01843 862 091

© DT

Feature

99 problems but a beach ain't one

Thanet's beaches have something for everyone, as IsleOne's Gareth Harris explains.

There's much to recommend Thanet: a thriving cultural scene, more and more good places to eat, oh, and did you notice that massive art gallery that's sprung up in Margate? So far, so good. But, massive art gallery aside, is there anything you can't find elsewhere in the UK? Well, consider the beaches…

There are 15 beaches and bays on the Isle, stretching from Ramsgate Main Sands up and around to Minnis Bay. A hugely impressive nine of these received a Blue Flag award last year. And while there are plenty of other destinations in Kent with beaches, not one of them has a Blue Flag. Thanet's got them all. Up yours, Whitstable.

34

As you'd expect, the main resorts are crammed during the summer. Throughout the holidays, Broadstairs' Viking Bay throbs with locals and lobster-pink Londoners alike. But just round the corner, past the tidal pool, lies Louisa Bay, inexplicably deserted except in the busiest weeks, where kids dig holes in the hard sand, families brew tea in their beach huts, and the only noise is the distant sound of a few show-offs titting around on their jet skis.

The only drawback to Louisa Bay is that the beach tends to disappear at high tide. But if you happen to find it submerged, park up at the excellent Louisa Bay Café (see **32**, page 30) on the promenade where you can sit and wait with Thanet's best bacon sandwich while the tide retreats.

Heading the opposite way out of Broadstairs you'll find Stone Bay. Often described as the locals' beach, it's notable as the venue for some hugely competitive beach-hutting. There are a few down there more luxuriously furnished than my house. But there's a drawback: Stone Bay loses the sun early, and at high tide is little more than a concrete strip.

In contrast, further up the coast at Kingsgate is Botany Bay, one of Britain's most picturesque beaches. Ignore the posters currently promoting Kent to hassled city commuters – it's not really populated by 20 year olds doing tai chi as the sun sets behind them. But the pair of gigantic chalk monoliths that rise up out of the sand are undoubtedly dramatic. Pass between them to the second, larger beach – it's almost always empty and you'll find rock pools for crabbing and caves in the cliff face. It gets cut off at high tide, so don't say we didn't warn you.

Visit in late spring or early autumn, when the Isle is empty but the weather is warm, and every beach feels like it's your own. The bays at Minnis and Westbrook, in particular, offer acres of space and seclusion. In winter, a cathartic trudge along the coast into the teeth of the wind is surprisingly rewarding. Good walks at this time of year are from Broadstairs to Ramsgate, through the unappealingly named Dumpton Gap, finishing off at the Belgian Bar (see **50**, page 48) for a hot chocolate or a cold beer. Alternatively set off from Joss Bay around Foreness Point, the most northerly part of the coast, all the way to Walpole Bay.

Keep going and eventually you'll end up in Margate, finishing up where it all began. Margate is reputedly the first ever British seaside resort – the place where beach holidays were invented. Since Turner, artists have journeyed here for the light; since Coleridge, poets have come to find inspiration on the sands; and since even before Chas'n' Dave, Londoners have travelled down, first by steamer then by high speed trains, for the air, the food, and the beaches. Plus ça change.

Broadstairs

© DT

38 Lillyputt Minigolf

Minigolf at the seaside is part of the same tradition as deckchairs, donkey rides and knotted hankies for hats. While you might not see too many hankies and donkeys on Thanet's glorious beaches these days, you can still enjoy a thoroughly authentic round of minigolf. Lillyputt is 12 holes of pure nostalgia, complete with a spinning windmill and the chance of a free game by ringing the bell at the end. Overlooking the sea above Louisa Bay, Lillyputt also serves food throughout the day. Their teacakes have even been featured on BBC One's Songs of Praise. Hallelujah! *(GH)*

Victoria Parade, Broadstairs CT10 1QS
T: 01843 861 500
Lillyputt.co.uk
Open weekends only during winter

Stay

39 The Victoria Hotel
It's not an exaggeration to say that The Victoria has the best position in Broadstairs: in the middle of town, but facing directly out to sea, past the lawns and bandstand of Victoria Gardens. Anyone expecting the typically Edwardian facade to give way to an interior of swagged fustiness is in for a surprise: owner Helen Kemp has created a coolly contemporary haven, all serene, pale colour palette and huge, sink-into beds. And the first floor sitting room, fully stocked with games, magazines and DVDs, has a balcony framing That View. It's where breakfast is served too, made to order from local produce. But book early: there are only three (lovely) rooms. *(MO'L)*
23 Victoria Parade, Broadstairs CT10 1QL
T: 01843 871 010
TheVictoriaBroadstairs.co.uk

40 Belvidere Place
Calling Belvidere Place a B&B does it a disservice: Jilly Sharpe's lovely Georgian townhouse minutes from the beach is more of a boutique hotel. Rooms are decorated with vintage finds and there are Egyptian cotton sheets on the luxurious beds. The sitting room (with toasty stove for cold days) leads onto an attractive courtyard garden where guests can have breakfast on sunny days. And those breakfasts: local produce, fat bangers, home-made fruit compotes… Too bad that Jilly – a knowledgeable, warm and immensely welcoming hostess – doesn't do dinner. Yet. There's not much of a view, but that's the only downside. At the vanguard of the new seaside cool. *(MO'L)*
Belvedere Road, Broadstairs CT10 1PF
T: 01843 579 850
BelviderePlace.co.uk

41 Number 68
In a world increasingly populated by boutique B&Bs with ornate antique beds and expensive art on the walls, it's easy to overlook places like Number 68. Choose from three themed rooms –French, Chinese and Seaside, if you were wondering – and wake up to a wonderful, locally sourced breakfast that even includes fruit from owner Mike Clarke's allotment during the summer months. Mike's also a fountain of knowledge when it comes to the local area. Perfectly placed for a long walk along the cliffs to Ramsgate, or the late-night schlep home from Broadstairs' bars and restaurants. *(ST)*
68 West Cliff Road, Broadstairs CT10 1PY
T: 01843 609 459
Number68.co.uk

Festivals and events

The Thanet calendar boasts a rich and varied programme of annual festivals. Here's our pick of the bunch.

Pushing Print
Pushing Print gives artists a platform to exhibit their printmaking, and encourages the public to get involved in the process. Launched in 2009, it became an instant hit, with submissions coming from as far away as America by its second year. A hugely popular Giant Print event, which sees steamroller printing on the road, as well as talks, workshops, and above all, world class artwork, are just a few of the reasons for its success. Real artists passionate about their craft, hands-on fun and a chance to be creative have led to this event becoming a firmly established fixture in the Margate Old Town calendar. *(A-MN)*
Last three weeks in October, 2011
Margate Old Town, various venues
PushingPrint.co.uk

Thanet Beer Festival
It's always good to find an excuse to experience Margate's Winter Gardens, perched like a huge wedding cake just past the Turner gallery on the edge of Cliftonville. A leaf through the listings is likely to reveal anything from a cut-price TV psychic to an appearance by chart-topping boyband JLS, but perhaps the best way to see it is through a pair of ale goggles at the Thanet Beer Festival. We could tell you to cast aside your preconceptions and keep an open mind, but we won't: the beards and beer bellies are out in force, along with chicken in a basket, and several hundred gallons of good, honest ale. *(ST)*
22 & 23 April, 2011
Winter Gardens, Margate
EasterBeerFestival.org.uk

Dickens Festival
Never has the expression "What the Dickens?" seemed more appropriate. Walk along Victoria Parade in June and you'll find a town swamped with enthusiastic thesps trussed up in their finery, parading the Broadstairs streets in bustles, bonnets and other mainstays of Dickensian dress. There's a packed programme of plays, readings, bathing parties and croquet on the lawn, and with a bit of luck Bleak House – once a museum, but now millionaire jeweller Richard Hilton's family home – might even be open to the public for a few days. The festival dates back to 1937, when Dickens House owner Gladys Waterer plugged a production of David Copperfield by persuading townsfolk to don period dress. *(ST)*
18-24 June, 2011
Broadstairs, various venues
BroadstairsDickensFestival.co.uk

Broadstairs Folk Week
Whatever your views are on Morris dancing – and it's a subject that can be quite divisive – Broadstairs Folk Week is about far more than a few men in funny costumes. The town is taken over entirely by musicians and music-lovers: bands play gigs at venues all over town or just set up wherever they find room. There are daily concerts and games for children, and there's an infectious party vibe throughout the town. The torchlight procession that opens the festival is bizarre, magical and unmissable. Arrange your accommodation early because every B&B and guesthouse is booked months in advance. *(GH)*
5-12 August, 2011
Broadstairs, various venues
BroadstairsFolkWeek.org.uk

Summer Squall
Last year's inaugural Summer Squall in Ramsgate was a huge hit, with attractions like the mesmerizing Sonic Junk Machine, a huge, moving orchestra fashioned from household junk and carted around on an electric milk float, among the exhibits delighting the crowds. Other treats included a solar-powered cinema, and a 'Ramsgate's Got Writing Talent' competition, with local literary types Jane Wenham-Jones and Iain Aitch becoming the Isle's very own Amanda Holden and Simon Cowell for the afternoon. The second installment looks to be every bit as quirky, engrossing and enjoyable. *(ST)*
August Bank Holiday weekend, 2011
Various venues
RamsgateArts.org

Harbour Arm Postcard Auction
Fancy picking up a Tracey Emin original at a bargain price? That's exactly what one canny bidder came away with in last year's charity postcard auction. Each September, on Margate's Harbour Arm, a scattering of celebrities put postcard-sized artwork up for sale in the name of a good cause, and the artist remains a mystery until the bidding's over, meaning you have every chance of getting your mitts on a star-scribbled effort – or just a doodle by the talented but anonymous bloke who lives up the road. Go steady at the Lighthouse Bar during the interval, or you just might just get carried away. *(ST)*
Saturday 11 September, 2011
Margate Harbour Arm
MargateHarbourArm.co.uk

Broadstairs Food Festival
A wonderful addition to the Broadstairs calendar, despite the odd entrepreneurial hotdog stall attempting to crash the party. Where else could you kick off with a deliciously strong, spicy Bloody Mary and bourgeois bacon sarnie courtesy of Age & Son, before hitting the rather civilized champagne bar, then wander off to witness a cookery demo by the likes of Dev Biswal, Thanet's very own celebrity chef? With the best of the Isle's artisan cheesemakers, bakers and brewers lining up to take part, the Broadstairs Food Festival looks set to grow and grow. *(ST)*
30 September – 2 October, 2011
Victoria Gardens, Broadstairs
BroadstairsFoodFestival.org.uk

Ramsgate

'Café Culture' was a buzz phrase much loved by a previous council leader, trotted out whenever the topic of regeneration came up. But just for once it's come to pass. The area around the country's only Royal Harbour has been transformed in recent years with a pleasing mix of bars, restaurants and pavement cafés opening up opposite the marina, bringing colour and vibrancy to the town.

All to the good, for Ramsgate has much to offer the discerning visitor with its fabulous architecture, sweeping Regency crescents, and tucked-away squares. It's a place steeped in history, with tales to tell that include the waving off of men to the Napoleonic Wars and sending the Little Ships forth on their rescue mission to Dunkirk.

Ramsgate has a strong connection with the arts, boasting a plethora of blue plaques marking connections with luminaries from Van Gogh to Wilkie Collins, John Le Mesurier to Frank Muir. Those who live here now are a rich mix too. An influx of Londoners has given the town a cosmopolitan flavour and led to the opening of specialist shops and some decent restaurants. It's all a far cry from the down-at-heel town that was the only place I could afford to live in my impoverished youth. Back then I swore hysterically I'd never live in Ramsgate again. I would now!

Jane Wenham-Jones

© Aaron Stone

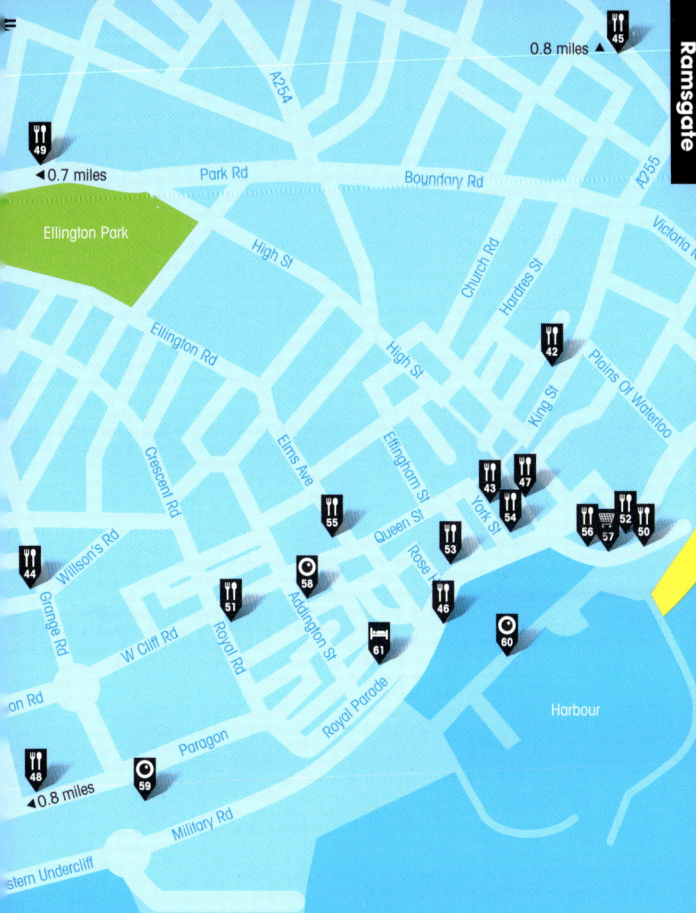

Ramsgate

- 45 ▲ 0.8 miles
- 49 ◀ 0.7 miles
- Ellington Park
- 42
- 43, 47
- 55
- 54
- 56, 57, 52, 50
- 44
- 51
- 58
- 53
- 46
- 61
- 60
- Harbour
- 48 ◀ 0.8 miles
- 59

Roads: A254, Park Rd, Boundary Rd, A255, Victoria Rd, High St, Church Rd, Hardres St, Plains Of Waterloo, Ellington Rd, King St, Crescent Rd, Elms Ave, Ellingtham St, Queen St, York St, Rose St, Willson's Rd, W Cliff Rd, Royal Rd, Addington St, Grange Rd, Royal Parade, Paragon, Military Rd, Western Undercliff

41

24 hours in Ramsgate

Artist and Ramsgate resident Susan Kennedy shares her tips for making the most of your time in the town.

Morning. Ramsgate's full of stunning Georgian architecture, giving even Bath a run for its money when it comes to the number of listed buildings. Find the best examples with a stroll around Liverpool Lawn, Spencer Square, Vale Square and Addington Street, where you can also spend an hour at the Pinball Parlour (see **58**, page 52). But it's not just the buildings that are impressive: residents and regular visitors to Ramsgate have included Jane Austen, Karl Marx, Queen Victoria, Elizabeth Fry, Dickens, Coleridge and Vincent Van Gogh, and you're never more than a few minutes away from a blue plaque. A walk along the west cliff's main promenade takes you past The Grange (see **59**, page 53), the hugely impressive former home of architect Augustus Pugin.

Lunch. Grab a light lunch in the old Custom House on the harbour, dropping in at Nice Things (see **57**, page 51) for a souvenir or two while you're there.

Afternoon. On a sunny day it's tempting to fritter away the hours in one of the Harbour Parade's pavement cafés, but make the effort to reach Ramsgate's Blue Flag beach and get some of that golden sand between your toes with a walk under the cliffs. Then stroll back to the harbour to watch the beautiful steam tug Cervia being lovingly restored by a committed bunch of volunteers. Head into the tiny Sailors' Church which nestles at the foot of Jacob's ladder, the steep stairs that lead you up onto the west cliff, perhaps ending the afternoon by heading out on a boat for a spot of seal-spotting (see **60**, page 53) – or even heading back to one of those pavement cafés.

Dinner. You're spoilt for choice for a decent dinner in Ramsgate. Head to Age & Sons (see **43**, page 44) or Eddie Gilbert's (see **42**, page 43) and you can't go wrong.

Evening. The Belgian Bar (see **50**, page 48) is a Ramsgate institution – a little tatty around the edges but a true one-off. Sample some of the 100-strong range of Belgian beers and some live music – more often than not you'll find a folk band belting out songs from the tiny stage.

Sleep. Housed in one of Ramsgate's magnificent Georgian crescents, The Royal Harbour Hotel (see **61**, page 53) has wonderful views of the harbour, the yacht marina and across the English Channel. Bath? You can keep it.

Food & Drink

© DT

42 Eddie Gilbert's
Since adding an upstairs restaurant to its award-winning fishmonger and gourmet chippy around the corner from the Royal Harbour, Eddie Gilbert's has had Thanet gourmands enraptured with its huge plates of locally sourced fish, and proper, dripping-fried chips. Don't miss out on the signature dish of soft-boiled duck egg with crispy, deep-fried eel soldiers; so good Observer food critic Jay Rayner named it his starter of the year in 2010. Wash it down with a bottle of Black Pearl Oyster stout, specially created for the restaurant by Ramsgate microbrewery Gadd's. Food doesn't come much more comforting than this. (ST)
32 King Street, Ramsgate CT11 8NT
T: 01843 852 123
EddieGilberts.com

Ramsgate

43 Age & Sons
Up a narrow alleyway minutes from the Royal Harbour, this stylish Victorian warehouse comes as a very welcome surprise, especially in the summer when the courtyard outside is populated with tables, umbrellas, even rugs for the evening chill. Chef Toby Leigh worked for Heston Blumenthal, and his daily-changing menus could feature vast chunks of roast Kentish beef for sharing – with 'thrice cooked chips', or seasonal dishes from fat artichokes, to slow-roast lamb with sea beets, to milts (don't ask). You can have the full celebratory blowout upstairs, or just a latte and cake in the café bar on the ground floor. A wonderful addition to the area. *(MO'L)*

Charlotte Court, Ramsgate CT11 8HE
T: 01843 851 515
AgeandSons.co.uk

44 The Conqueror
Pubs don't come more pint-sized than The Conqueror, the young upstart of Thanet's increasingly busy real ale scene; just 15 people can park their spare tyres at the counter. Drop by and sample beers from local breweries like Gadd's, Wantsum and regular guests from more distant climes. There's a sweet story behind all those barrels of bitter, too: the pub gets its name from a paddle steamer that used to make trips between Ramsgate and Boulogne at the turn of the last century. Landlord Colin Arris's granddad was the skipper, and first clapped eyes on his future wife, Colin's grandmother, on board. *(ST)*

4c Grange Road, Ramsgate CT11 9LR
T: 07890 203 282
Conqueror-Alehouse.co.uk
Closed Mondays

45 The Brown Jug
From the pétanque pitch in the beer garden to the bizarre clock hanging behind the bar with its twinkling on-the-hour tune, The Brown Jug is a place that inspires affection from the second you walk through the doors. Monthly meetings of the Writers Circle, piles of pub games, and a fabulously soppy German Shepherd holding court in the back bar are just a few of its many charms. There are open fires to keep you snug in the winter, regular quiz nights and the warmest welcome this side of the Wantsum Channel. *(A-MN)*

204 Ramsgate Road,
Broadstairs CT10 2EW
T: 01843 862 788

46 Ship Shape Café

If you threw a small bomb into a chandlery, the result might look something like this endearingly shonky joint. Hanging from the low, arched ceiling are everything from lifejackets to random plastic buoys, and every surface bristles with nauticalia. Sure, it's a greasy spoon, but a quality one: the ham that comes with egg and chips is home-baked, as are the cakes – try featherlight Victoria sponge, or coffee and walnut, a pound for a fat slice. Avoid coming out fragranced with bacon by joining the salty seadogs at outside tables looking onto the Royal Harbour. The sign on the door reads 'We aaaaargh open'. *(MO'L)*
3 Military Rd, Ramsgate CT11 9LG
T: 01843 597 000

Thanet dining: we're getting there

Feature

***Metro* restaurant critic and Thanet resident Marina O'Loughlin dishes the culinary dirt.**

When I first started coming to the Isle, you couldn't in all fairness describe it as a culinary paradise, unless you counted the acres of cauliflower and cabbage that scent the area with their distinctive fragrance at the end of summer. But fortunately, some talented chefs and restaurateurs have now made their home here, possibly drawn by the magnificent quality of the Kentish produce: meat, vegetables and fruit, plus some of the finest seafood in Britain.

Ramsgate has the pick of the bunch, with the celebrated Eddie Gilbert's (see **42**, page 43) and Age & Sons (see **43**, page 44). The former demonstrating that fish'n'chips and upmarket, assured cooking needn't be mutually exclusive, the latter delivering Flintstones-sized cuts of amazing local beef and proving that people can and will eat fish sperm: the milts are a regular feature on the menu.

Even the cafés are raising their game in response: it's a rare new establishment that doesn't trumpet local provenance (the cakes at Oscar's Festival Café (see **29**, page 29) are home-baked with Kentish eggs for example) or at least nod at seasonality. This might seem like basic stuff, but it's a giant leap for an area where the café's previous incumbent used to buy entire meals from the cash & carry up the road.

One thing we do lack is the kind of informal seafood shack that can be found routinely in places like Cornwall and Jersey. Why, I've no idea: Thanet's seas are teeming with lobster and crab, and those rude interlopers, American oysters: meatier and arguably more delicious than natives, are in season all year round. I have great hopes that once Camilla and Paul Naisbitt have settled into the Louisa Bay Café (see **32**, page 30), they might consider dishing up the odd plateau de fruits de mer. With its mesmerising view and a chilled bottle of something crisp and white, I can't imagine anything nicer. Or simply buy your own from Fruits de Mer on Broadstairs Broadway: with no exaggeration, one of the best fishmongers in Britain.

Of course, it's not all warm welcomes and Michelin pretenders even today: I'll gloss over the leather-chaired outfits who regularly have Brakes trucks parked outside. But these haven't found their way into this guide so hopefully you won't find them either.

Some, fortunately, are dying out, the best kind of natural selection. As we go to press, the hilariously bad House of Coffee in Broadstairs has been sold, with talk of a specialty teahouse replacing it. And rumour has it that Gary Rhodes, a Thanet College alumnus, is looking for premises on the Isle. Now that I would like to see.

47 Surin

This tiny restaurant garnered an improbable amount of positive press when it first opened. The Lao-Thai-Cambodian food was remarkably fresh and authentic, and owner Miss Damrong's background in chi-chi hotel and restaurant kitchens meant that Ramsgate had gained a bit of a star. These days, the scuffed interior could definitely do with a bit of love, but the food is still good: fiery larb gai (chicken salad), rich Penang curry, unmissable coconut sticky rice – perfect with the own-brand beer. The flavours may be exotic, but the produce is local – a beguiling combination. *(MO'L)*
30 Harbour Street, Ramsgate CT11 8HA
T: 01843 592 001
SurinRestaurant.co.uk
Closed Sundays

48 Belle Vue

While this charming little pub has a rich history – legend has it that Dickens once took Hans Christian Anderson for a few jars here – it won't win any awards for décor. But the sweeping vistas stretching around the coast from Pegwell Nature Reserve past Sandwich to Deal Pier more than make up for it. A quiet, serene spot for a couple of ales after a bracing walk around Pegwell Bay, there's also an open fire to warm your sodden socks upon in winter. Narrow smugglers' tunnels still connect the Belle Vue with the cottages up the road. *(A-MN)*
Pegwell Road, Pegwell Bay,
Ramsgate CT11 0NJ
T: 01843 593 991
TheBelleVueTavern.co.uk

49 Newington Fish Bar

The Newington Fish Bar is a conundrum. It's one of those subjects that can divide families and set communities at war. The issue here is whether it is permissible to have fish and chips in a polystyrene container. For the purist, only paper will do; for the pragmatist, polystyrene is acceptable. Probably the best advice for this wonderful award-winning chippy on the outskirts of Ramsgate is to eat in or eat them quick: whatever you do, don't close the lid or the crispy batter surrounding the juicy white fish will go soggier than a wet weekend in Whitstable. And who wants that? *(GH)*
55 Newington Road, Ramsgate CT12 6EW
T: 01843 591 549
Closed Sundays

Ramsgate

© DS

50 Belgian Bar
All mussels and murals, the Belgian Bar is a haphazard arrangement of banquettes and tables where you can eat, drink and critique the local artwork covering every inch of the wall. The food is robust – a varied selection of decidedly un-Belgian roasts, paella and pasta alongside those moules – but perhaps not as robust as the 100 or so beers on sale behind the bar. If the artwork isn't your thing, you can always take a seat outside. The Belgian Bar's location overlooking the Royal Harbour makes it the perfect place for a spot of people watching – a highly evolved art form in itself. *(GH)*
98 Royal Parade, Ramsgate CT11 8LP
T: 01843 587 925
BelgianCafe.co.uk

51 The Artillery Arms

It's the Grade II-listed building that makes The Artillery worth a visit, with ornate stained glass windows mixing Napoleonic scenes with the names of long gone local breweries. A traditional boozer regarded by many as Thanet's best pub for real ale, it has all the features you might want from an authentic, old-fashioned pub – a regularly updated selection of ales, and regulars who've been frequenting the place since time began. Go if you enjoy sharing tasting notes on local and national ales like Gadds and Acorn Firecracker; don't go if your preference is for a Fosters Top. *(GH)*

36 West Cliff Road, Ramsgate CT11 9JS
T: 01843 853 282

52 Albion Café

It's the location of this tiny café that sets it apart from the crowd. Tucked at the top of Kent steps overlooking the harbour, on a sunny day it is flooded with light and, with only a handful of tables, a place to relax for a moment and enjoy the view. The interior exudes a faded charm, with walls covered in black and white photos of Ramsgate's glorious past. Then there are the huge portions of no-nonsense traditional British food (fry-ups, roasts, sandwiches and puddings) and equally no-nonsense prices. More than anywhere, this café seems to embody the very heart and soul of Ramsgate. *(AS)*

10 Kent Place, Ramsgate CT11 8LT
T: 01843 588 412
Closed Mondays

53 La Magnolia

Voted best Italian in the Kent Restaurant Awards back in 2009, this busy, family-friendly restaurant offers authentic Southern Italian cooking with spectacular views of the Royal Harbour. Try the Ramsgate-caught fish of the day, authentic wood-fired pizzas or the home-made, chargrilled Italian sausage. Simplicity is of the essence – fresh, clean flavours, topped with a dollop of genuine Italian hospitality. Book ahead for a window table or sit outside in the summer time and soak up the atmosphere. *(AS)*

9-12 Westcliffe Arcade,
Ramsgate CT11 8LH
T: 01843 580 477
LaMagnolia.co.uk

54 Corby's Tea Rooms

While a view of the Ramsgate branch of Wilkinson's can't compete with the Royal Harbour, and the décor is admittedly a little on the fussy side, Corby's remains an unpretentious delight. Friendly staff dish up a fairly standard selection of mains and snacks alongside delicious cakes and the obligatory cream teas. The people of Ramsgate head here in droves, and it's not unusual to see three generations of Thanetian huddled around a table together, or a flush of grannies enjoying a teacake or two. Bring a friend, bring the family or just bring a crossword. Corby's delivers everything you could ask and more from a traditional English tearoom. *(SK)*

18 York Street, Ramsgate CT11 9DS
T: 01843 586 078
Closed Mondays

55 Patogh

Tucked away anonymously between Waitrose and the Royal Harbour, this family-run restaurant is all too easy to miss. Ignore the exterior and English menu; it's the authentic, aromatic Persian food which makes Patogh one of the Isle's hidden gems. Chef Saeed works alone preparing delicious starters like kofteh berenji (meatballs with rice) and kashke badjeman (mashed aubergine), and mains like chargrilled meats, slow-cooked stews and jewelled rice fresh to order. In the summer months they even serve up canteen-style lunches through the kitchen hatch. Book well in advance for a seat at the bargain Persian buffet on the last Friday of the month. *(AS)*
2 Effingham Street, Ramsgate CT11 9AT
T: 01843 852 631
PatoghRestaurant.co.uk

56 Pelosi's

While the admittedly wonderful Morelli's in Broadstairs (see **33**, page 31) basks in the limelight, Pelosi's hovers in the background like a shy little sister. But don't overlook its less brash charms: Pelosi's is, in its understated way, a stunner: green vitrolite walls with curved mirrors, Germolene-pink chairs and ice-cream a go-go. For me, the quality of that ice-cream can outshine its flashier Broadstairs neighbour, somehow lighter, with brighter flavours: the pink grapefruit could wake up the doziest palate. And there's exotica like pomegranate or pistachio – a duo designed to match the pastel colour scheme. 'Established 1945' it says on the sign. Long may they continue. *(MO'L)*
76 Harbour Parade, Ramsgate CT11 8LP
T: 01843 593 585

Shopping

57 Nice Things

You could be forgiven for thinking that Margate's Old Town has the monopoly on arty gift shops, but Suzy Humphries and Bella Goyarts' shop through the terracotta-coloured columns of Ramsgate's domed Custom House is full to bursting with glorious paintings, ceramics, prints and jewellery. There's a constantly changing range of artwork showcasing talent from East Kent and beyond, and whether you're a serious art collector or a holidaymaker looking for a keepsake, there's always something to suit your budget. Stop by at the Custom House café to admire your purchases over a cup of tea, too. *(A-MN)*
Custom House, Harbour Parade,
Ramsgate CT11 8LP
Nice-Things.co.uk
Closed Mondays

See & Do

Ramsgate

© DT

58 Pinball Parlour
A 50-year-old pinball machine might seem technically primitive compared to an X-Box or PSP, but it's no less engaging. The Pinball Parlour houses around 20 vintage machines spanning most of the 20th century and represents a unique way to spend a couple of hours, whatever your personal vintage. Most of the machines are playable, and you can follow their evolution from flipperless bagatelles, via the introduction of ramps, multi-play modes and bonus levels, through to the electronic machines of the '80s and '90s. Proof that you don't need the internet to have fun. *(GH)*
2 Addington Street, Ramsgate CT11 9JL
T: 07966 217 295 or 07930 326 008
PinballParlour.co.uk
Open weekends only 1pm-6pm

59 Pugin's Grange

If you really want to do Ramsgate in style, how does a weekend staying in the old family home of 19th century Gothic revivalist Augustus Pugin grab you? He's best known for designing the grand interiors at the Palace of Westminster and the clock tower of Big Ben, but The Grange is the seaside bolthole Pugin knocked up for himself before allegedly succumbing to syphilis at the tender age of 40. Pugin loathed the uniformity of Ramsgate's sweeping Georgian terraces, to which the building stands in stark contrast. It sleeps up to eight people, or you can make do with the guided tour on Wednesdays instead. *(ST)*

The Grange, St Augustine's Road,
Ramsgate CT11 9PA
LandmarkTrust.org.uk

60 Seal Tours

Whether you want to bob around in a powerboat or kick back on a sports cruiser, taking to the water for a spot of seal watching is a thrilling way to experience the Thanet coastline. All budgets are catered for, so if you're eager to get up close and admire the wildlife or just peer down your nose while sipping chilled champagne, you'll find just the vessel you need. If seals aren't your bag, you could always take a trip out to inspect the futuristic wind farm instead. Galleon Cruises cater for the more luxurious end of the market, while Horizon offers a full range of tours and packages. *(GH)*

Horizon Sea Safaris, Royal Harbour,
Ramsgate. T: 07931 744 788
HorizonSeaSafaris.co.uk
Galleon Cruises, Royal Harbour,
Ramsgate. T: 07740 071 015
GalleonCruises.com

Stay

61 Royal Harbour Hotel

Few hotels in the UK can match the elegant Royal Harbour Hotel when it comes to location – on a clear day you can even see France while propped up on the pillow in your four poster bed. Cobbled together from a row of smart Georgian townhouses, the Royal has a sunny sea-facing terrace for the summer months, and comfy sofas, an honesty bar and a roaring fire for those bracing Thanet winters. The love scene from 2008 Bob Hoskins hit Ruby Blue was filmed in Room 23, and to keep the celluloid link going, proprietor James Thomas has installed a cute 20-seat cinema in the basement for private screenings. *(ST)*

10-12 Nelson Crescent,
Ramsgate CT11 9JF
T: 01843 591 514
RoyalHarbourHotel.co.uk

Elsewhere

Typically one thinks of Thanet as Margate, Ramsgate and Broadstairs. But in fact the district covers over sixty square miles and stretches out through Westgate and Birchington to Sarre Mill in one direction, and Minster and Cliff's End in the other.

Explore the Isle of Thanet and you'll not only encounter all walks of life, but every sort of landscape too. From the ever-changing coastline to the flat cabbage fields, from river to sea, hamlet to town, endless rooftops to leafy greenness, you will see council estates and des res splendour, drive-thrus and corner shops, high rise blocks and tiny flint cottages.

Wind your way around the Isle's roads and you're as likely to meet a horse as a sailing boat, a runner or cyclist as the driver of a Jag. There are many here who have never lived anywhere else and never would. Newcomers find how friendly it is. And how ever so slightly strange. Like a much-loved mad old aunt, Thanet is a place of eccentricity, quirk and foible. And just when you think you've seen it all, it's still full of surprises.

Jane Wenham-Jones

© Jo Tammaro

Food & Drink

62 Carlton Cinema and Frederick's

Mother and daughter owners Joanna Cornford and Charlotte Russell took a leap of faith by taking on the three screen Carlton Cinema. The extraordinary building has been in the family since the 1940s and the cinema celebrates its 100th birthday next year. Frederick's, named after Charlotte's grandfather, is bliss: original cornicing, door handles and stained glass all adding to its charm. Joanna makes the soup, scones and quiches, while Charlotte is responsible for the irresistible cakes. She says daughter Iris was the inspiration: she smelled like lemon cake when she was born. *(MO'L)*

23 St Mildred's Road,
Westgate-on-Sea CT8 8RE
T: 01843 834 290
CarltonCinema.com

© DT

Elsewhere

63 Botany Bay Tea Garden

Afternoon tea in a beautiful English country garden, listening to the soft tones of Mozart being played on the piano? Don't mind if I do. And all the cakes are homemade? Lovely. Botany Bay's dramatic chalk stacks are often used as the 'Face of Thanet', and an hour at the Botany Bay Tea Garden is the perfect way to round off your site seeing trip. One of Thanet's best-kept secrets, Alison opens up her father's walled garden every summer to serve divine cakes and other fabulous high tea accompaniments. Both dogs and children welcome, last house on the left by the beach. *(A-MN)*

165 Botany Road, Broadstairs CT10 3SD
T: 01843 867 662
Open Thursday – Sunday from April until the end of summer

64 Quex Barn

The sprawling Quex Estate is something of a Free Range multiplex. The farm shop sells delicious meat from beasts that mooed their way around the grounds just days before, as well as local fish, vegetables and Kentish wine. The café does one of the finest breakfasts in Thanet, and you can even sit at your table gazing at the hens that laid the eggs you're about to tuck into. If your tastes extend beyond a cooked breakfast, The Hannah Dining Suite offers fine dining within the four grand walls of Quex House. Explore the Powell Cotton Museum (see **67**, page 58) while you're here. *(GH)*

Quex Park Estate, Birchington CT7 OBB
T: 01843 846 103
Quexbarn.com

65 Westbay Café

There's no shortage of little cafés to park up at along the Viking Trail cycle route from Reculver to Ramsgate, and the promise of an OAP's roast washed down with a mug of Bovril from this café's menu is less than enticing. But one thing guaranteed to get the kids onside is a hefty portion of chips served up in a bucket. Your own brand new shiny bucket full of chips to munch away at while dreaming of the castles you'll create. They even throw in a spade, too! It stays open late, and makes a great spot for taking in that beautiful Thanet sunset. *(A-MN)*

The Promenade, Sea Road, CT8 8QA
T: 01843 831 791

Shopping

© DT

66 Brocante

Dawn and Rob Rigden-Murphy's off the beaten track shop – it's up a side street in less-travelled Westgate on Sea – is well worth tracking down for anyone who enjoys a rootle in antique and vintage shops. They go on regular buying trips to the Continent (and, no, they're not about to give away their sources) coming back with vanloads of goodies – chandeliers made of antlers or fashionable armoires or forties' Perspex side-tables. Some are be stripped and painted into elegant pieces, some left *au naturel*. You know those expensive shabby chic stores in London? This is one of their suppliers. But we didn't tell you that, okay? *(MO'L)*
23 Ethelbert Square,
Westgate-on-Sea CT8 8SR
T: 01843 831 171

See & Do

Elsewhere

67 Powell Cotton Museum
Shooting and stuffing the native wildlife as he made his way around Africa and Asia in a pith helmet and safari suit, Victorian explorer Percy Powell-Cotton brought a whole new dimension to souvenir hunting. Truly one of a kind, the Powell Cotton museum is packed with mementoes from an age that broke all the rules. The jaw-droppingly awesome panoramas allow you to get up close to giraffes, bears, rhinos and elephants, and there's more than enough to keep any child or adult utterly spellbound. Don't miss the exquisite gardens, and take a tour around neighbouring Quex House too if it's open. *(A-MN)*
Quex Park, Birchington CT7 0BH
T: 01843 842 168
QuexMuseum.org
Check website for opening times

68 The Hornby Visitor Centre

Hornby has a long and illustrious history in Thanet. Their latest contribution is an interactive museum with models from as far back as 1921, including the original clockwork O gauge locomotive. But it's not all model railways: over the years Hornby has acquired several big names in the toy world, and there are displays for other big brands like Scalextric (yes, you can have a go), the eternally spoddy Airfix, and Corgi. And in case you were wondering, the exit and entrance are via the well-stocked shop. An hour well spent, particularly for children of the '70s. *(GH)*
Westwood Industrial Estate,
Margate CT9 4JX
T: 01843 233 524
Hornby.com/VisitorCentre
Open Wednesday – Sunday
£4/£2

69 Monkton Nature Reserve

Tucked away down a track on the site of an old quarry you'll find a tired old prefab building. Ditch your preconceptions, because inside is a joy to behold: casements of skulls, fossils, and carefully preserved bird wings you can pick up and handle, referenced by carefully typed or handwritten cards. Knowledgeable, friendly staff are happy to identify any curious bits of rock, shell or fossil you've found while beachcombing too. If the kettle's on, have a cup of coffee and leaf through the huge collection of second-hand books. A real blast from the past. *(AS)*
Monkton, Ramsgate CT12 4LH
T: 01843 822 666
Monkton-Reserve.org
Call for opening times

70 Spitfire Museum

The kind of place you'll find full on a cold and wet January afternoon, the Spitfire Museum buzzes with the infectious murmuring of visitors, enthusiasts and volunteers enjoying the morale boosting wartime songs drifting from the speakers and reflecting on the war. Two big planes dominate the small, carefully curated rooms, and there's an excellent café that's just perfect for rounding off your visit. On a sunny day you can even take your food into the gardens and watch the modern day flying machines coming in to land at neighbouring Manston Airport. *(A-MN)*
The Airfield, Manston Road,
Ramsgate CT12 5DF
T: 01843 821 940
SpitfireMemorial.org.uk

To Thanet

Trains
Impressive-sounding high-speed Javelin trains link London with Thanet, regularly serving Margate, Broadstairs and Ramsgate from St Pancras. You can opt to take the coastal route via Whitstable and stop at Margate first, or go via Canterbury and hit Ramsgate first. Bear in mind that they're only high-speed until you reach Ebbsfleet or Ashford.

London – Margate takes around 1hr 30m
London – Broadstairs takes around 1hr 24m
London – Ramsgate takes around 1hr 17m
An open day return currently costs just shy of £40

Alternatively you can pick up one of the slower services from London Victoria, London Charing Cross or London Bridge, saving around £5 in the process. Journey times vary between just under a couple of hours to 2 and a half hours, depending on where the trains stop en route. For timetables, service updates and tickets visit SouthEasternRailway.co.uk.

Coach
The coach is well worth considering if you're on a budget, with a day return ticket costing around £10 less than the train, and the travelling time not too much longer. National Express runs five coaches a day to Margate, taking around 2hr 30m. An open return ticket costs just under £25. The same service continues on to Broadstairs (add 15 mins) and Ramsgate (add 25 mins), stopping at Birchington, Westgate on Sea, Cliftonville and St Peters too. For timetables, service updates and tickets visit NationalExpress.com

Road
The drive to Thanet takes just under a couple of hours from southeast London on a good day. Getting over the Dartford Crossing is usually the slow bit – from then on it's plain sailing down the A2 and M2.

Plane
Thanet is served by the rather grandly named Kent International Airport in Manston. Flybe has daily flights to and from Edinburgh and Manchester.
For tickets and prices visit ManstonAirport.com

Around Thanet

Transport

Taxi
Taxi is by far the most convenient way to hop between the Isle's main towns. Central Cars has offices in Margate, Broadstairs and Ramsgate, and offers a fairly reliable service. Here's a rough idea of what you can expect to pay.

Margate – Broadstairs: £6.00
Broadstairs – Ramsgate: £5.00
Margate – Ramsgate: £7.00
Central Cars: 01843 833 333

Bus
The Thanet Loop, run by Stagecoach, covers all of the Isle's main towns. A Dayrider ticket costs £2.70 and gives you unlimited journeys in Thanet. For timetables, service updates and tickets visit Stagecoachbus.com

Train
Regular trains operate between Margate, Broadstairs and Ramsgate, calling at Birchington, Westgate on Sea and Dumpton Park too. A trip between any of the stops shouldn't take any longer than 15 minutes, but at over £3 a ticket it's well worth taking taxi if there's more than one of you.

Bike
Cycling is a great way to explore Thanet in the summertime. The Viking Coastal Trail winds all the way along the coast, taking in sandy beaches, dramatic cliffs and cute villages. Hire a bike from Caitlin's Beach Cruisers (see **04**, page 8) if you can't be bothered bringing your own.

Car
Nowhere's very far away in Thanet. On a good day it should take no more than 10 minutes to make the trip between any of the Isle's main towns by road.

Contributors

Iain Aitch
Iain Aitch was born and raised in Margate, leaving at the age of 18 and pursuing a career as an author and journalist. He has written for the Guardian, Times, Daily Telegraph, The Idler, Dazed and Confused and Coast magazine. His most recent book We're British, Innit is published by Collins.

Ann Carrington
Ann trained as a sculptor at the Royal College of Art, and has won numerous awards, including the national competition to find a major new public artwork for Margate. Her bronze sculpture, Mrs Booth, is sited on the Harbour Arm. Ann works from her studio in Margate, and exhibits in London and New York.

Kiki Case
Committed urban girl now converted seaside dweller, Kiki Case is a freelance writer, blogger, editor and co-founder of Isle, a listings and features magazine for Thanet. When she's not writing, she can be found revelling in the sand dunes, sea breeze and salty air of the East Kent coast.

Gareth Harris
Since moving to Broadstairs with his family, Gareth has completely failed to find a single crab in a rockpool even though the coastline is supposedly teeming with crustaceans. When not elbow-deep in seawater and bitterness, he runs IsleOne.co.uk, Thanet's leading (and only) blogazine.

Susan Kennedy
A founding member and Chair in 2010 of Ramsgate Arts, Susan is an active participant in the Thanet arts scene and has exhibited her own work at The Pie Factory in Margate. She loves living in Thanet and rates the local community, the arts scene and chips in a bucket as highlights of the area.

Julie Marson
Julie moved from Fulham to Broadstairs for love eight years ago and is an enthusiastic convert to coastal living and Planet Thanet in particular. A former City banker, in the days when you could admit to it without issuing a grovelling apology, she now enjoys a totally wholesome life as wife, mother, magistrate and freelance writer.

Anne-Marie Nixey
Anne-Marie Nixey left her suffocating job as a teacher in the city to set up a new life in Thanet with her business Qing Art. Passionate about Margate Old Town she has worked tirelessly to get it the recognition it deserves and to allow others to enjoy all that Thanet has to offer.

Marina O'Loughlin
Marina O'Loughlin has been reviewing restaurants anonymously for over a decade. She has twice been voted one of London's Most Influential People (by the Evening Standard) and was seventh in BBC Olive Magazine's list of the most decadent foodies of all time – ahead of Henry VIII.

Ann Scott
Ann moved to Ramsgate from London almost five years ago and is passionate about the area. She set up her own graphic design and publishing company, PatrickGeorge, 18 months ago with her husband and contributes to raising the profile of the arts and culture scene in Thanet with unbridled enthusiasm.

Peter Scott
Peter has over 20 years experience in graphic design and illustration. Since starting PatrickGeorge, his illustrations have appeared in various publications including GQ, The Times, The Big Issue and in corporate publicity campaigns for companies such as Dell. He designs and illustrates children's books and is committed to the Thanet arts scene. Visit www.patrickgeorge.biz for more info.

Contributors

Denis Smith
Denis is a Ramsgate based photographer. He worked in London as an Art Director and after leaving Saatchi's moved to Ramsgate to pursue his passion of the photographic image. He feels equally at home in the studio or on location, and loves the variety in his assignments.

David Thomas
David lives between Thanet and Holborn. His photographs have been used by the BBC, The Telegraph, Coast magazine, and extensively in online guides.

Stewart Turner
Stewart is a travel and TV journalist who has written for the Guardian, Time Out, BBC.co.uk and Orange.co.uk. He moved to Cliftonville from London a couple of years ago after falling in love with Margate's stunning architecture and glorious sandy beaches, and is passionate about promoting the Isle to the unconvinced and unconverted.

Jane Wenham-Jones
To date, Jane Wenham-Jones has spent 95% of her life with a Thanet address although she makes sure she escapes the Isle sufficiently frequently to fully appreciate its joys on her return. Jane is an author and freelance journalist whose columns include a regular slot as 'Plain Jane' for the Isle of Thanet Gazette. For the full low-down visit JaneWenham-Jones.com